# Moments Of Madness

## 8 Zany Short Comedies For Our Times

By

Jack Berry

Published by Blue Moon Plays

For Your Once-In-A-Blue-Moon-Experience

**Special Considerations:**

**Small-group readings around a table or in the classroom:**

- If you are planning to use this script FOR CLASSROOM USE, you must purchase scripts for the members of your class or group. These may be purchased as a downloadable PDF (class/group study pack) which may be printed for that class only.
- If you are a small group doing private play readings for YOUR OWN ENTERTAINMENT or for a SMALL SENIOR ACTIVITY GROUP, you must purchase the number or scripts required by the characters: these may be purchased as a multi-copy download which will give you a printable script that you may copy for that reading only.

Digital versions cannot be added to a free or paid online library or website, in any format, with or without member access without the publisher's permission.

## TO PERFORM THIS PLAY

**You must buy sufficient scripts for the cast + 3, apply for performance rights, pay the performance fee, and receive a performance license.**

**To purchase scripts:**

- Purchase sufficient printed hard copies (one for each cast member, plus 3 for the crew) - an automatic 10 percent discount is applied to multiple printed hardcopies at the point of ordering.

**or**

- Purchase a Multicopy PDF which allows you to print sufficient copies of this script (one for each cast member, plus 3 for the crew). Click Return to Merchant to download your printable PDF. A link to the download will also be emailed to you, along with a link to the application for performance license.

**To apply for a Performance License**, go to the Product Page of the play and fill out and submit the application form.

**To pay the Performance Fee**, simply pay the invoice you will be emailed when we receive your application for performance.

**Your Performance License for your requested dates will be emailed to you.**

All scripts and licenses shall be obtained at Blue Moon Plays at
www.havescripts.com


**If you wish to make changes in the script of any kind, you must receive
permission from the publisher or the playwright. Permission is usually granted
readily when schools or theaters face casting problems and the changes do not
affect the quality or intent of the original.**


**For information, visit** www.havescripts.com;
**email** info@bluemoonplays.com
**or  call 757-816-1164**


Individual plays within this collection can be ordered as downloadable, printable
PDF's (Multicopy Performance) on the site for productions. Please follow the
guidelines

# Contents

# Anecdotal Evidence

Characters:   SIMON/SERGEANT/HOMEOWNER  (male, any age)

FISHERMAN1/SOLDER1/FOP1  (male, any age)

FISHERMAN2/SOLDIER2/FOP2 (male any age)

Props:     2 Helmets, 2 police-like caps, 2 FAKE Rifles, Binoculars

Setting:   Begins with New Testament Israel, continues to WW I Trench, concludes with  contemporary suburban street

At rise:  FISHERMAN1 & FISHERMAN2 are at Stage Right (SR), SIMON is just off Stage Left (SL)

FISHERMAN1 (peering incredulously towards SL):   Is that who I THINK it is?

FISHERMAN2:  Simon!

FISHERMAN1: The Leper.

FISHERMAN2:  You know he hates that name – "Simon The Leper".   I wouldn't like it either.

FISHERMAN1:  We BOTH know other Simon's – it's the easiest way to tell the difference between them all and it's not like we have to worry about his feelings – he's UNCLEAN.

FISHERMAN2 (To FISHERMAN1, as SIMON enters from SL):  Doesn't look like it now, though...

SIMON (clothed only from waist down):  It's a MIRACLE!   I met Jesus of...

FISHERMAN1: Nazareth – there's only one Jesus worth talking about.

SIMON: Right! He cured me of my leprosy! He told me to bathe in the Jordan and look at me! (FISHERMAN1 and FISHERMAN2 approach him cautiously). LOOK AT ME! I haven't been this clean since I was a teen!

FISHERMAN1: And this happened after bathing in the Jordan?

FISHERMAN2: I didn't know the Jordan could clean anyone. It looks pretty gunky, if you ask me.

SIMON: It wasn't the Jordan! It was JESUS! I've been in the Jordan plenty of times and it didn't do squat for me. But Jesus told me to do it so I figured "what the hell". And now I'm so shiny – head, toes, and hiney.

FISHERMAN1: So just based on that, you're jumping to the conclusion that it was Jesus? That's just one data point.

FISHERMAN2: Actually, I heard about him turning the water to wine at a wedding.

SIMON: He's got game – I saw him heal the lame.

FISHERMAN1: That's anecdotal evidence.

SIMON: If YOU don't wanna believe, that's your business. But I believe! And you know what the BEST thing about this is?

FISHERMAN1: We don't have to worry about bumping into you?

SIMON: OK, the SECOND-best thing about this.

FISHERMAN2: What?

SIMON: I don't have to hear about you calling me "Simon The Leper"!

FISHERMAN2: I didn't call you that...

SIMON: Word gets around...

FISHERMAN1 : I think I might've called you "Simon The Leopard" one time – you know – because you were so agile in your early days.

SIMON: Yeah, right — you think I was born yesterday? Well, ok, actually, I was RE-born today. But I HAVE feelings! I didn't like being DEFINED as a leper. Would you like being called "Bart The Whiner"? Yeah, I heard about that (mocking whiney voice) "Waah… I don't have back support".

FISHERMAN2: It was a long sermon and that fish kid just would NOT sit down in front.

FISHERMAN1: Sorry, man — no hard feelings…I wasn't the only one …

SIMON: I FORGIVE you — that's what Jesus…

FISHERMAN2: Of Nazareth?

SIMON: YES! Of Nazareth! Yeesh, stay focused… eye on the prize. He'd want me to forgive you.

FISHERMAN1: I promise that we won't call you that anymore and we'll correct those that do.

FISHERMAN2: Especially as it's not even applicable. But what should we call you? "The Simon formerly known as Leper"? That's too long.

SIMON: You'll think of something. (very moved) I get to come home. (really sinks in) I get to go home. Thanks to His Amazing Grace, I can show my Face (exits SR).

FISHERMAN1 (has an idea for name): And there goes Rhymin' Simon…

(FISHERMAN1 and FISHERMAN2 stare off at SR, amazed at what they saw).

SIMON (hurriedly back from SR hands FISHERMAN1 and FISHERMAN2 each a helmet and rifle): Trust me, you'll need these. (SIMON exits SR again).

(FISHERMAN1 is now SOLDIER1, FISHERMAN2 is now SOLDIER2, SIMON is now SERGAENT and still off SR).

SOLDIER1 (puts helmet on, crouches, aims rifle at SL, squeezes his neck): Another cramp…nothing like trench warfare.

3

SOLDIER2 (puts helmet on, crouches, aims rifle at SL): I hear ya – "Great War" -- for WHO?   Great WASTE is what it is.

SOLDIER1 (mockingly): On the bright side, this will be the war to end all wars.  Not that I'll live to see that.  If it's not the bullets, it's one disease or another.

SOLDIER2: All this because ONE  arch-duke gets bumped off.   What's an arch-duke anyway?

SOLDIER1: I guess he was someone's arch-enemy.   Wilson should've listened to George Washingtion – avoid foreign entanglements.

SOLDIER2:  He also warned against forming political parties, right?

SOLDIER1: Yeah, a real smart guy.   But we didn't listen & now we'll never see home again.

SOLDIER2:  One day at a time – let's try to stay sharp...

SERGEANT (enters from SR with binoculars): Hey, stay sharp!   (peers thru binoculars):   Uh... is that what I think it is?   Just when I thought it couldn't get any worse...

SOLDIER1:  What?  What?   I don't see any enemy advance!

SOLDIER2:  Me neither?   Sarge?

SERGEANT:  I can only PRAY it's not what I think it is...

SOLDIER1:  What?  What?

SERGEANT:  Gas.

SOLDIER2:  It wasn't ME this time and the rations are terrible.   You're just as bad.

SERGEANT: From the Germans!   I was hoping it was just a rumor but they're using mustard gas.   It will make you WISH you were dead if you breathe it.

SOLDIER2 (panicking):  What do we do?  What do we do?

4

SOLDIER1: I can see it now!   We don't have any masks, right?   What do we do?

SERGEANT:   I know this is gonna sound weird but wee on your shirt and hold that to your face.   It's crude but the ammonia works.

SOLDIER2: My shirt?  Isn't that disrespecting the uniform?   That's a court-martial offense.

SERGEANT: Any piece of cloth – whatever you can find.   It'll save your life!

SOLDIER1: What?   That's outrageous!

SERGEANT: Just telling you what I've heard from other units.

SOLDIER2: So we're relying on anecdotal evidence?

SOLDIER1: Has this theory been thoroughly tested?

SERGEANT: Do you have any alternative?   We're gonna die otherwise! I'm gonna do it – just gotta tell the others about it – we don't have masks and we're out of options! (runs off SL).   Do it!

SOLDIER1: It's just someone pulling a prank.   I'm not gonna go out this way.

SOLDIER2:   It's on (cough) us – I can't (cough) breath!

SOLDIER1: Let's fall back (cough) – I'm having trouble seeing!   Can't (cough) shoot what you can't see!

SOLDIER2: Fall back!  Fall (cough) back!   I can't see either!  (runs off SL along w/ SOLDIER1):

SERGEANT (back on from SL with shirt being used as a mask, surveying the chaos):   And there's our double-blind study (runs back off SL).

(nobody on stage, as SERGEANT becomes HOMEOWNER, SOLDIER1 becomes FOP1, SOLDIER2 becomes FOP2).

(FOP1 and FOP2 form a mini "conga" line and enter from SL, wearing caps and making various siren sounds – this part should be very silly):

5

FOP2: A wooh, woooh, woooh! (best attempt at siren sound)

FOP1: Baah Baah Baah! (best attempt at siren sound)

FOP2: Bee dop!   Bee dop! (another attempt at siren sound)

(Both stop in mid-stage)

FOP1: What are you doing?

FOP2: Whaddaya mean?

FOP1: Pick a siren sound and STICK with it!

FOP2: It got people off the streets and out of our way, didn't it?

FOP1: We're PROFESSIONALS.   We lose credibility when we improvise on the siren.

HOMEOWNER (rushes onto stage):  Thank God you're here!   The fire is out of control in the woods and is heading towards my house!  (stops and sees that FOP1 and FOP2 don't look like firemen).   Uh, wait -you guys aren't firemen – are you COPS ?

FOP1:  We're not cops either.

FOP2:  We're Fops!

HOMEOWNER:  What?   What is that?

FOP1:  FOPS.    Fauci's Overbearing Police State.

HOMEOWNER:  Never heard of you guys but I see you DID bring a truck.  Hydrant is, thankfully, just to the left of my property line.    I'll let you guys get to work.

FOP2: It looks like a mostly peaceful fire.

FOP1: How did this all happen?

HOMEOWNER: I don't know – was minding my own business, looked out the window, saw this fire that looked to be burning out of control in the woods back there between my house and the street back there.    What difference does it make?   I need you to put it out!

FOP2:  Maybe the neighbor on the street back there did it to burn some leaves.

HOMEOWNER:  No!   We didn't start the fire.   Can you hook up your hoses and put it out now?   Hurry before the fire gets to my house!

FOP2:  Hoses?

HOMEOWNER:  For the water!   So you can douse the woods.   Right?   That's what you do!   Right?

FOP1:  We know how to do our jobs.

HOMEOWNER:  Then do it!   Douse the woods!

FOP2:  With water, you say?

HOMEOWNER (exasperated):   Yes, Yes!   You put the fire out with water – it's clearly not electrical – just a brush fire!

FOP1:  We KNOW what kind of fire this IS, sir!

HOMEOWNER:  Then put it out!

FOP1:  Easy now – don't shoot the messenger.

FOP2:  We're the experts at this sort of thing.

HOMEOWNER:  Then what are you waiting for?

FOP1 (condescending):  So you think water will put it out?

HOMEOWNER (very frustated):   Uh, yeah!   That's how these fires are put out – with water – it happens all the time.

FOP2:  That's anecdotal evidence.   (mockingly)  I heard of a guy who got cleared of leprosy by bathing in the Jordan river.

FOP1:  Yeah, we can't just act on every "theory" that a homeowner has. Water has never been tested as a fire retardant in a carefully controlled, peer-reviewed double-blind study.

HOMEOWNER:  We don't have TIME for this!  My house will get burned. But, PLENTY of houses have been saved by water!

FOP1:  That doesn't mean anything.   It could be the fire would've died out on its own.   In order to PROVE that water was the solution, you'd have to randomly choose some woods on fire and douse them  and the other woods on fire you'd not use any water.   Otherwise, you're not controlling for the placebo effect.

HOMEOWNER:  What?  Do you see how ridiculous that is?   You're fiddling while Rome is burning.

FOP2:  Rome is not in our precinct.

FOP1:  You also have to make sure that the home owner doesn't know if his house is on fire or not – that's why we call it a double-blind study. Oh, and the FOPS or fire department shouldn't know either.

HOMEOWNER:  Well I know that my house will burn to the ground unless you do something.   I highly recommend that you hook up your bleeping hoses to that bleeping hydrant over there and  drench the woods.   DO YOUR JOB!

FOP1:  Maybe you shouldn't have moved to a neighborhood where the houses were so close together.

FOP2:  Yeah, that was pretty irresponsible – it just takes one match & then you have a conflagration.

HOMEOWNER:  I'll THINK about it after this is over!    Now, DO YOUR JOB!

FOP1 (looks at cell phone):   Relax, man – our models show the fire heading way from your house and dying out.

HOMEOWNER: (Runs towards SR and looks towards back stage):   Huh (very relieved).   It does seem to be heading away and, yeah, it IS dying out.

FOP1:  See?  Nothing to worry about.   We're professionals – we know what we're doing.

FOP2 (to HOMEOWNER):  I think SOMEONE here owes us an apology.

HOMEOWNER (to neighbor back stage):   Oh, you called the Fire Department?   Great work!   I don't know how it got started either!   Thanks, man!   (back to FOPS).   See?   He called the fire department, they doused the fire with water, and now the fire is OUT.   So putting the fire out with water WORKED.

FOP1:   Hey, if you wanna give credit to the water, I guess I can't stop you.

FOP2:   You'll  probably post it on the internet but it's STILL just anecdotal evidence.

FOP1 (To FOP2, primarily):   I don't know why EVERYONE thinks they should tell us how to do our jobs.   They just need to trust the experts.

# A DARK DAY FOR HINKLEY, J.

Characters:   SUPERVISOR: Male/Female in charge of a mental hospital 40-60 years old SPECIALIST:  Female psychologist 20-30 years old.

JOHN:  John Hinkley Jr., attempted assassin of Ronald Reagan

Setting:   A small office or conference room within a mental hospital   At rise, SUPERVISOR and SPECIALIST are talking and JOHN is offstage.

SUPERVISOR:  I know you're new to this facility and haven't met all our patients but we have a crisis with one and you're a specialist so here's a chance to earn your money.

SPECIALIST:  Who's the patient?

SUPERVISOR (looking down at clipboard) NJ1981 -- Hinkley, J.   Goes by the name "John" these days.

SPECIALIST:  What's the crisis with him?

SUPERVISOR:  You're young so this was before your time but he tried to kill President Ronald Reagan back in 1981.   He also shot two or three others, paralyzing one, James Brady, for the rest of his life.

SPECIALIST:  Yes, I'm familiar with his case, though I don't know all the details.

SUPERVISOR:  He was declared innocent via insanity and he's been in this place for a long time – before I even got here.   I've done some homework on him.   He hasn't raised any flags over the last few years and even has a girlfriend, Leslie, from what I can understand.

SPECIALIST: So you need me to step in because...

SUPERVISOR: We haven't had to adjust his meds and he has even made it to the #2 spot on the pool challenge ladder. But today...

 SPECIALIST: He's obsessed with reaching the #1 spot? Well, having a goal can be a good...

SUPERVISOR: NO! That's not it at all. Did you read any of the entertainment news yesterday?

SPECIALIST: I thought we kept those magazines just for the patients. I've got better things to do.

SUPERVISOR: Maybe you should start. Anyway, Jodie declared she is a lesbian.

SPECIALIST: Jodie who? I thought you said his girlfriend is named "Leslie." Oh, there's some sort of love triangle you need me to resolve.

SUPERVISOR: Wow, you really are young. John did the whole shooting thing to impress Jodie Foster. He fell in love with her, watching "Taxi Driver".

 SPECIALIST: Bob James

SUPERVISOR: What?

SPECIALIST: He did the theme song – very pretty – it's where Tony Danza and Danny Divito got their starts, right?

 SUPERVISOR: NO! That was the TV series "Taxi". "Taxi DRIVER" was a movie. Jodie was 12 years old. John fell in love with her, stalked her, and attempted to kill the President to try to impress her. That's why he's here. Now after all these years, Jodie has come out as a lesbian and someone has to break the news to John.   We have NO idea how he'll react – that's why we need YOU, you're the specialist at dealing with disappointment resolution.

 SPECIALIST (big exhale):  Tough way for me to start here but it IS what I do.   Where can I find him?

 SUPERVISOR: I'll send him in right now.   (SUPERVISOR leaves, returns, and brings in JOHN)
 John, this young lady is here to help you.   You can trust her.   She has some news for you.   I'll be out in the hall if either of you need me.   (SUPERVISOR leaves):

SPECIALIST: (warmly)   Hello, John!

JOHN (very guarded):  I'm here because Soapscum said I cheated at pool, right?

SPECIALIST (a bit taken aback):   I haven't met the patient you call "Soapscum".

JOHN:  Everyone calls him that.   But I came up with the name after the bathroom incident.

SPECIALIST:  Bathroom incident?

JOHN:  One of the newbies couldn't find the bathroom.   I told him to use the process of elimination.   I'm very creative. (sullen) Not that it matters around here.

 SPECIALIST:  I'm sure you are.   No, this is about something else.   I've heard you've become proficient at using your tools to handle disappointment.

JOHN: I didn't burn the cue stick when I scratched on the 8 ball.

12

SPECIALIST:  That's very impressive.   But this is about something else.

JOHN:  Jodie returned my last letter!   That's it, right?

SPECIALIST:  Now, you know she hasn't wanted to read your letters in a long time but ...

JOHN:  How else will she know how much I love her?

SPECIAIST:  But that shouldn't matter because you have Leslie now.

JOHN: Leslie says it's the Nazi party's loss for kicking me out.   Bunch of wimps.   I should've realized it when they said NEO Nazis.   Don't fix what ain't broken.

SPECIALIST:  The important thing here is  that you've developed a support system.   So I think you'll be a trooper when I tell you the news.  How do I put this – it seems Jodie, uh, is not on the team we all just assumed she was on.

JOHN:  Jodie joined the Nazi party?

SPECIALIST:   Um, no.   She never liked them.

JOHN:  But my love could've conquered and overcome that!   She just doesn't understand love.

SPECIALST:  Um by "other team", I mean something different...

JOHN (suspicious):  Yeah?

SPECIALIST: Now, remember your coping tools....

JOHN (more suspicious):  I don't like where this is going.

SPECIALIST:  It seems that Jodie is a lesbian.

13

JOHN:  Why?  You thought she was flirting with you?

SPECIALIST: No, we've never met.   But you get the internet here, right?

JOHN: Yeah, but it's real slow.   Who do you have to kill here to get Road Runner?

SPECIALIST:  I wanted you to find out before reading the story on the computer.   Jodie IS a lesbian.

JOHN (stunned):  That can't be!   I've seen her in all her movies and she always liked men!   Even that guy in "Silence of the Lambs" -- and he was creepy.

 SPECIALIST:  This is the shock part of grieving.    It's how we all start.

JOHN:  Didn't you think he was creepy?  Yet she liked him so she can't be a lesbian.   I mean, wow his voice was SO irritating.

SPECIALIST:  OK, you're in denial now.   But let's forget about the movie and focus on YOU.

JOHN (angry):  How could she DO this to me?   She betrayed me!

 SPECIALIST:  Anger.   That's natural.  I have to say you're making tremendous progress – better progress than some of the people here who don't get promotions, in fact.

 JOHN:  If she just would read my letters!

 SPECIALIST:  Bargaining... we're almost there now.   Bring it on home, John.

 JOHN:  I'm gonna STRANGLE her for making a fool of me – they won't let me have a gun.

SPECIALIST: OK, that's a step back... but let's use our tools.  All those years that she didn't want you, well, she didn't want ANY men!  And so...remember what we've taught you ...

JOHN:  Blue pill before red, just before bed?

SPECIALIST:  Well, that's always good to know.  But more specifically about this news.

JOHN:  Just because things don't go my way, I shouldn't take it personally?

SPECIALIST:  Exactly!  And?

JOHN:  I now have closure and can resolve my ambivalence towards my relationship with Leslie?

SPECIALIST (very pleased with progress): Yes!  Yes!  And you know something, John?  I actually think that Leslie is prettier than Jodie anyway.  So you see how everybody wins?

JOHN:  I think the James Brady family is still cheesed off at me, though.

SPECIALIST:  Yeah, some people are funny that way.

# Employee of the Month

Characters:  JEFF, male any age shopper at big department store

RANDY, male 20-40 who works at store

MARY,  female co-worker of RANDY, roughly same age as RANDY

GROVER, store manager (male or female), preferably older than RANDY/MARY

   Props:  Cell phones for RANDY and MARY, small shopping bag for JEFF

Setting:  Large Department Store


At rise,  JEFF is casually shopping (MARY and GROVER are off-stage) and RANDY runs to catch up with him

RANDY:  Uh, sir...sir?    SIR!

JEFF:  (puzzled):  Me?

RANDY:  Yes, you.    Now, we don't want to cause a scene, excuse me... what's your name?

JEFF (hesitatingly): Uh, Jeff.

RANDY (into cell phone):  Customer's name is "Jeff".   I think I can handle this without security but be ready just in case.  (to JEFF): OK, Jeff, there's no need to make this unpleasant – especially if you don't have a criminal record.

JEFF:  Of course, I don't!   What is this about?

RANDY (into cell phone):   Can you verify this, Travis, based on facial and first name?    I THINK he'll be reasonable about this.

JEFF:   Reasonable about what?

RANDY:  I mean, please don't make a run for it.   (into cell phone) Travis, your team has already sealed the exits, right?    I COULD tackle him but I'd prefer not to.   Yeah, this time it's the LEFT shoulder (back to Jeff):   This should be over pretty quickly if you cooperate.

JEFF:  Could  you please tell me what's going on?    I was just shopping like anyone else.

RANDY:   Anyone else?    Hardly, sir.   We don't want to embarrass you so we won't make you watch the security camera tape.    (into cell phone):   We've got it all on tape, though, right, Travis?

JEFF:   Got what on tape?

RANDY:   (into cell phone) You have to HOLD the gray button. (back to Jeff): Please don't make me spell it out for you – you know what you did.

JEFF:   No, I don't!

RANDY (into cell phone):  CLAIMS he doesn't know what he did (beat).    Guess we'll do it  the hard way.    (to JEFF):   Aisle 7... last chance, Jeff – we have audio and video.

JEFF:  Not a clue.

RANDY:  (into cell phone):  It's a twister – category three, at least. (To JEFF): You farted in the bedroom section, Jeff.

JEFF (incredulous):  What?   That's it?

RANDY:  The sign says "comforters" but just because you're a paying customer does NOT mean you can trash our place.   Would you do that at home?

JEFF:  Well, yeah, all the time.

RANDY: OK, bad example.   At a friend's house?

JEFF (thinks about it):  Depends on the friend.

RANDY:  That's very disrespectful to your friend but THIS is criminal.   Our pillows, surface rugs, quilts have all been compromised.    Honestly, would you buy a pillow knowing that someone had uh, well you know...

JEFF:  I'd just take another one that hadn't been uh,... "compromised".

RANDY: TAINTED.    Yes, you would – because you VANDALIZED some of our merchandise.   Now, if you'd just gone a few more feet into, say, the lawnmower section, nobody would care.   But you didn't – and now we have merchandise that we, in good conscience, cannot sell.   Unlike the on-line companies, WE have integrity.

JEFF:  What if I buy the top quilt and pillow?

RANDY:  We still have to disinfect the rest of the items with a special spray.  Who's gonna pay for the spray?

JEFF:  I'll pay for the spray.

RANDY (to cell phone):  Discount for bulk still on?   Good!   (to JEFF):  If you buy three cans, you can keep two for yourself & still get the discount.   Handy around the house ... you'd actually be getting a bargain.

JEFF:  Whatever it takes to get me out of here.

RANDY: So that would be 2 quilts, 2 pillows and those 4 surface rugs – the ones on the top of the stack.   And the 3 cans.   Would you like the protection plan?

JEFF: Protection plan?   What could go wrong with this stuff?

RANDY: No, protection plan in case you go shopping here again and, uh, some of the food doesn't always agree with people – you wouldn't be the first --so you wouldn't have to pay any moneys should a similar incident occur.   You've saved a lot on the bedroom stuff so no point being  penny-wise and pound-foolish.

JEFF (resignedly):  Sure.

RANDY: You're free to go then – all the merchandise is up front (JEFF exits and  MARY enters from opposite direction):

MARY (shaking her head in admiration):    You're an ARTIST!

RANDY:  Couldn't have done it without your help, Travis.

MARY: I'm sure  THAT one puts you over the top.

RANDY:  I THINK I had it clinched without that one but it's nice to have some cushion.

MARY: So you've now won Employee of the Month every month since I've been here.

RANDY:  Which hasn't been long at all, though, right?  Two months or so....

(GROVER walks in)

GROVER: You won it last month but we're discontinuing it till further notice.

RANDY:  Why?

MARY:  What?  You should at least give him THIS one.    He earned it!   He worked really hard.

GROVER:  That would be two in a row and would not reflect the values we're trying to represent.

RANDY:  What are you talking about?

MARY:   Uh-oh, I see where this is going.

GROVER: You're clearly a white male, Randy – no Native American heritage, right?

RANDY:  I've lived here all my life if that helps.

GROVER:  You know what I mean.

RANDY:  I've never even left the country!

GROVER:  Answer the question:   Any Native American heritage?

RANDY:   For all I know, I COULD have ...

MARY:  Better be honest, Randy – you've SAID you'd never run for political office but you may one day change your mind.

RANDY:   OK, as far as I know, I do NOT have any.

GROVER:  And you're clearly not gay.

RANDY:  How do you know that?   Not that I am but...

GROVER:  I've seen you flirting with Mary the last two months.

RANDY:  I wasn't flirting!   I was just...

MARY:  You were flirting – it just wasn't GOOD flirting – it was way too...

GROVER:    I could tell it was flirting and I was halfway across the store.

RANDY:  I just wanted her to feel welcome as a new employee.

GROVER:  Yeah, right.

MARY:  Two months in?

RANDY:  So am I in some trouble for that?

GROVER:  Relax, there's no harassment that I know of.  Mary?

MARY:  Of course not.  I thought it was all pretty funny.  He kept calling me by last name for one thing.

RANDY:  Just trying to keep it professional.  It sounds cool when they do it on "NCIS."

GROVER:  Back to my original point, though – You're a straight white American male.

MARY (To GROVER):  Maybe he hasn't always identified as a male.

RANDY:  I took cooking classes a few years ago.  And I like watching chick flicks.

GROVER:  Didn't help you with your flirting, apparently.

MARY (To RANDY):  And your name is gender-neutral.  But have you always had a...what's the politically correct word these days?

GROVER:  An "Outy".  You've always had an "Outy", right, Randy?

RANDY:  Yeah, pretty sure about that .  Mary?

MARY:  Always had an "inny".  Just because I know a lot about lawn mowers?  Wow, this flirting has sunk to a new low.

RANDY:  That's not what I was gonna ask you.

GROVER:  So there you have it.  You're not giving me anything to work with.  We simply cannot have a White American Straight

Always Male win Employee of the Month twice in a row.    It sends the wrong message.

RANDY:    That we reap what we sow?

GROVER:    That we're not embracing diversity.

RANDY:    How about if I credit Mary with my last three sales? Then SHE would be Employee of the Month.    That would give us diversity.

MARY (very touched to RANDY):    You'd do that?

RANDY (To GROVER)    She did help me a lot.    So that would work, right?

GROVER:    No, because it looks even worse – two months in a row to the same INTRA-racial and straight married couple.    Eww.

RANDY:    We're not married!    We haven't even been on a date...

MARY:    Yet.

GROVER:    You two WILL be.    I've been doing this a long time and all the signs are there.    Look, I gotta make corporate happy.    Just live with it, Randy – life is full of disappointments – do you really think MY dream was to be manager here?    (GROVER walks off briskly, as he sees a potential crisis elsewhere)

RANDY (yells out to GROVER):    I always assumed it was!    (MARY laughs at this).

MARY:    That's a complete rip-off that you didn't get the award this month.    Just because he didn't wanna look politically incorrect.

RANDY:    You know, I kinda hate to make him look bad about the other thing.

MARY:    What other thing?

RANDY: About US one day, uh....don't we OWE it to our manager to at least see where it goes?

MARY: You really are bad at this flirting thing – are you asking me out?

RANDY: I'm TRYING. But I wanted to do it after winning Employee of the Month – that way we could go to a real nice place.

MARY: I thought you took some cooking classes. Did you forget what you learned?

RANDY: Hey, right now it's hard to remember everything because just being near you is intoxicating.

MARY: Now, THAT's a pretty good line. Grover give it to you?

RANDY: Nope, thought of it myself.

MARY: Impressive!

RANDY: It took me two months. Well, one month for the line itself – another to figure out how to work it into the conversation.

MARY: You're an artist. Our shift is just about over... hey, do you see that guy in aisle 8?

RANDY: Yeah, he looks like the kind of guy who would...

MARY: Go get him, Randy. Travis has got your back.

RANDY (briskly walks off stage). Excuse me... Sir? Sir? We don't want any trouble...

# Not Your Fairy Godmother

Characters:   JUAN, male/female adult

               DEUCE, male/female adult

               TRACY, male/female adult

               FARM HANDS INSURANCE COMPANY (FHIC), male/female adult

               BIG BROTHER GOV (BBG), male adult, preferably bigger than others

Props:  Thirty quarters or half dollars, green felt representing a lawn, 2 cell phones

Setting:  Suburb in the U.S.

(At rise, JUAN is down stage, FHIC is up stage, others are off stage):

JUAN (Surveys the stage, stretching his back, talking to himself): The lawn is looking good.

DEUCE (enters from stage left):  Nice lawn, Juan...Zoysia?

JUAN: I don't have time to molly-coddle.  Centipede.

DEUCE: Hey, I'm getting a few tests done tomorrow.

JUAN: On your lawn?  What for?  Bunch of weeds.  We all know that.

DEUCE:  No, on ME.  I feel fine but some of the numbers are concerning and I don't wanna one day just up and...

JUAN:  Drop dead.

DEUCE:  Right.

JUAN:  No, I mean DROP DEAD.   I know where you're going with this. We're neighbors, Deuce, but we've never been CLOSE friends or anything so, no, I'm NOT gonna help you pay your medical bills.   I've got my own problems  (DEUCE walks off stage right discouraged as TRACY enters from stage right).

TRACY:  Nice lawn – looks like you put in a lot of effort.

JUAN:  Yeah, pretty back-breaking work, Tracy.

TRACY:  I hear ya.

JUAN:  No, I mean BACK-BREAKING.   I'd go to Physical Therapy but I'm not made of money... any chance you could...

TRACY:  You should've spent less time and effort on your lawn just so you could impress your neighbors.   Get bent (walks off stage left and FHIC saunters towards JUAN).

JUAN: (yelling out after TRACY as he flexes his back):  That's my problem – I can't straighten out!

FHIC:  I see this problem a lot.

JUAN:   Who are you?

FHIC:  Farm Hands Insurance Company.    But you can call me "Insurance Company" for short.   I can help you.

JUAN (suspicious):  Yeah, right.

FHIC:  Just give me 9 pieces of silver and I'll pay for most of your medical expenses for the next year.

JUAN:  What's the catch?

FHIC: Well, there's a co-pay for each visit until you meet your deductible.

JUAN: I knew it! I'm gonna need a lawyer to figure it all out. "Meet my deductible?" Is that like my "spirit guide" or something?

FHIC: No! It's just our terminology for making sure you have some "skin in the game". We just wanna make sure you don't just see doctors willy-nilly.

JUAN: They're just down the street! Willy seems to be pretty sharp. Nilly is a quack, I agree.

FHIC: What I mean is that we just don't want someone seeing a doctor at the drop of a hat.

JUAN: Maybe it's early Parkinsons or some other muscular thing...

FHIC: I mean FRIVOLOUSLY. That's all we ask – be responsible with your visits and we can cover you – especially if we can do a group rate.

JUAN: That seems fair (yells out): Hey, guys! Check this out (DEUCE and TRACY re-enter stage). Meet "Insurance Company".

FHIC (extends right hand to shake): Farm Hands Insurance Company is my full name. But I'm fine if my clients call me "Insurance Company."

DEUCE: We're not your clients – at least I'm not.

FHIC: Just 9 pieces of silver from each of you and you're all covered for the year.

TRACY: Does that include dental?

FHIC: Uh...

TRACY: I knew it! It's like pulling teeth to get good coverage.

FHIC: For another piece of silver, I'll do dental.

DEUCE: That sounds pretty reasonable. I'm your client.

TRACY: I'm in!

FHIC: OK, your policy numbers are: One, Two, and Three (addressing JUAN, DUECE, TRACY in order)

ONE: Great, he's given us all numbers and taken away our names.

FHIC: It just speeds up the claim process. We value you all as individuals, though.

(JUAN, DEUCE, and TRACY, each enthusiastically give FHIC 10 pieces of silver, shake hands, walk off stage happy)

FHIC (to himself alone on stage): Thirty pieces of silver – what could possibly go wrong? I'm living the dream. (singing to his silver as he fondles the coins): Oh, my darlings, oh my darlings...(no longer singing but talking to them as if they're his children): I love EACH and EVERY ONE of you. Let's see who's the shiniest. Everyone line up – you all are such good kids.

DEUCE (re-enters): Hey, I've got an MRI tomorrow and it's gonna cost me four guys.

FHIC (talking to his silver): I knew (sob) that this day would someday come so we have to say goodbye to three of you. (gives 3 pieces of silver to DEUCE). Here you go – we're paying 75%.

DEUCE: Fair Enough! Thanks, Insurance Company! (takes his 3 silver pieces and exits happy):

FHIC (alone on stage again talking to silver): Every parent's nightmare is that his child won't outlive...

JUAN (re-enters): My back is still killing me. I gotta go to Physical Therapy. It's one guy...

FHIC (hands him 1 piece of silver): OK

JUAN: Per visit.

FHIC (suspicious): Yeah...

JUAN: They want me to come three times a week for two weeks. So that's six visits, which equals six guys (holds out hand expectantly).

27

FHIC (hands JUAN 5 more pieces of silver).   I really hope your back feels better soon.

JUAN:  Thanks, Insurance Company – you're the best (is about to leave when TRACY shows up):

TRACY (to FHIC):  I went to Derm.

FHIC:  Where did you get shot?

TRACY (puzzled at first):  Huh?   Oh.... Dermatology!   Not Durham. Nothing too serious but a freeze-off.

FHIC:  Location?

TRACY:  Tenth Avenue.

FHIC:  No!   Where on your body did they have to freeze off?

TRACY:  On my face.

FHIC:  So it's cosmetic then.

TRACY:  But I told them I was picking at it  --- which I WAS on the drive over -- and they said you'd cover it.     It's only two guys (FHIC hands over 2 more pieces of silver).

DEUCE (re-enters):  Now they wanna do a cat scan!

FHIC (resignedly):  Doggone it (hands over 3 pieces of silver).

DEUCE:  Thanks, Insurance Company.

JUAN:  That reminds me – I'm also seeing a chiropractor.

FHIC:  Your personal life isn't really my business.

JUAN:  No, I mean as a PATIENT – twice a week for the next four weeks.

FHIC:  All this from maintaining your lawn?

JUAN:  Oh, no, I decided to see if I could jump my neighbors trash cans with my motorcycle.

TRACY: And I cut myself moving the trash cans and went to the E.R recently (holds out hand to FHIC)

DEUCE: That reminds me – they wanna do more blood work. (holds out hand to FHIC)

JUAN: I'm not as young as I used to be and I've recently discovered that getting eye doctor appointments can be a pain in the rear. (holds out hand to FHIC)

TRACY: Hindsight is twenty-twenty.

FHIC: Stop it! I can't keep shelling out money to you all!

TRACY: But your name is "Insurance Company"! That IS what you DO, right?

DEUCE: Yeah, what do you think we pay you for?

JUAN: What a rip-off! We should go to the guy downtown. Silas Marner Insurance Company! I think he'd do right by us. That's what the commercials say.

FHIC: Maybe you should all google FGM Insurance.

TRACY: I will! (gets busy with cell phone).

FHIC: Find it?

TRACY: I can't find it.

DEUCE: Me neither.

FHIC (very sarcastic): And you wanna know why? Because Fairy God Mother Insurance doesn't exist! They went out of business when gummy worms no longer became accepted as currency.

JUAN: Yeah, well, you're, uh... Greedy Evil...uh...Step...Mother Insurance. We gave you 30 pieces of silver and all we've gotten back...uh... I think I got nine.

DEUCE: I got seven

TRACY: I got eleven.

JUAN: Anyone got a calculator?

TRACY: Geez, just use the associative rule of addition.

DEUCE: Commutative.

TRACY: No, ASSOCIATIVE. So that's only twenty-seven pieces of silver. Meanwhile you're just sitting there fondling your THREE pieces of silver and singing to them.

FHIC (embarrassed): You saw that?

TRACY: Yeah, there's not much here in the way of props. You're a BAD Insurance Company!

DEUCE (scolding FHIC): BAD Insurance Company!

JUAN (to FHIC): You suck!

FHIC (sobbing): I'm not a bad Insurance Company. I've got kids, adjusters, overhead. That's where the three silver guys go!

BBG (enters on stage): Hey, I couldn't help but overhear...

TRACY: Insurance Company here has been bawling pretty loudly. Where did YOU come from?

BBG: I've been around forever.

JUAN (to BBG very reverently): You're MUSIC. And YOU write the songs.

DEUCE (to BBG): Did you take the Eighties off?

TRACY (to DEUCE): I hear you disparage Eighties music all the time but the fact is that that decade had some terrific music. It wasn't all hair bands and self-indulgent videos.

DEUCE (not impressed): Uh-huh.

TRACY: Ah-ha!

DEUCE: Ah-ha what?

30

TRACY: Ah-ha.

DEUCE: WHAT is your point? If you say "Ah-ha!", you gotta have a point.

TRACY: My point IS Ah-ha! They were fantastic and they came out of the eighties so you can't just dismiss the eighties. And some of the seventies music was pretty poor – I could give you examples of...

BBG: I'm NOT Music!

JUAN (crestfallen): Oh. Then who are you?

BBG: I'm Big Bro Gov.

TRACY: So you haven't been around "forever."

DEUCE: What a creepy... (to BBG): When DID you get here?

BBG: Around 1984. I'm here to give everyone insurance. Go ahead and get with the times and ditch Farm Hands Insurance Company. Put 'em out to pasture!

FHIC (sniffling): I'm a GOOD insurance company, I am.

BBG: Big Bro Gov is here to save you.

TRACY: Aren't you too busy investigating each other?

BBG: Ask not what you can do for your country but...

TRACY: Besides pay taxes and die fighting wars halfway around the world to save tribe A from tribe B?

JUAN: Maybe we should give Big Bro Gov a chance.

TRACY: Uh, aren't you guys Trillions of dollars in debt?

BBG: Gotta spend money to make money.

DEUCE: And if we had a problem with you, who would we talk to?

BBG: Click on our web page and that will direct you to our app.

JUAN: I don't know about you guys but I really like a live representative.

DEUCE: It's hard to get a live representative for PHONE service these days.  Anyone see the irony?

BBG:  No.

TRACY:  I do.

JUAN:  Is that a heavy metal band?

TRACY (to BBG):  The four of us – I'm including Farm Hands Insurance Company – have worked hard all our lives.  Didn't we also give you a lot of money for Social Security that whole time? Enough so that we'd be millionaires by now if we'd just invested it ourselves at five percent?

BBG: That's an over-simplification.   We live in a global economy.  (trying the Jedi mind trick) These aren't the facts you're looking for.

TRACY:  And if we don't like what you're doing, where else could we go? Another government?

DEUCE:  That's it – we don't need you, BBG.   We've got Farm Hands Insurance Company!

FHIC:  You mean it?   You're staying?

JUAN:   We LOVE you, Insurance Company!   We're sorry about saying that you suck.

DEUCE (to FHIC):  We meant "suck like a popsicle".  So it was a compliment.

TRACY (to FHIC):  And if you DO eventually hose us, we can always go to Silas Marner.

JUAN:  Or FGM.

TRACY:  That was a fictitious company, remember?   It never existed.

FHIC:  Happy to have you back but... uh...just a suggestion.   How about you all  cut down on the weekly bungee jumping?

JUAN: Hey! It's OUR Saturdays!

TRACY: Everyone's working for the weekend.

DUECE (muttering): Eighties crap.

FHIC: Could you at least wear a helmet from time to time?

TRACY: You drive a hard bargain, Insurance Company.

# RTFM

Characters:   Major Tom (MT), male astronaut

Ground Control (GC),  male


Props:   Protein bar, control panels, helmet, manual in a big loose-leaf binder


Setting: MAJOR TOM is at Stage Right chewing leisurely on a protein bar, separated from GROUND CONTROL at Stage Left


GC:  Ground control to Major Tum.

MT: It's "TOM", not "Tum!"  How many times do I have to tell you that?

GC: Irritable today – did you take your protein tablets?

MT: Yes.  (under his breath) Protein bar is the same thing.

GC:  Protein bar is NOT the same thing.   We gave you tablets for a reason.

MT: They taste chalky.   (starts putting helmet on)  In answer to your next question, my helmet is on.

GC: Engines are on.    Did you check ignition?

MT:  You just said the engines are on – doesn't that imply that ignition is on?

GC:  No, there's a difference – I can't believe you don't know that at this stage of the mission.

MT: Hey, all this science I don't understand.

GC:  Perhaps you should try and RTFM.

MT: (clueless) RTFM...uh, yeah, I'll get on that...

GC: Read the freakin` manual.  So do you really not understand the science or do you just like quoting Elton John?

MT: Bernie Taupin, actually.    A little of both, I guess.

GC: Important information in it!   Could save your life.

MT: I dunno -- learning about "lift" and "thrust" was a real drag.  But ok, I see here that we have ignition.

GC:  May God's love be with you – um, I guess I'm still allowed to say that – right, you're not offended by that, right?

MT: No, I'm cool with it, GC.   May God's love be with you too.

GC:  I know we've had our differences and I'll be honest – I really thought you'd wash out of the program.

MT:  Well, my dad is a senator on the right sub-committee so I was pretty confident that I wouldn't.   Good thing we don't have term limits, eh?

GC:  But this time you've really made the grade.

MT:  I'm still being graded on this?   Sounds pretty pass/fail to me. Either I come back alive or I don't.

GC:  My way of saying "good job."

MT: That's right, you're from England.

GC:  No, I'm not – I just like to say "blimey" if something goes wrong – nobody gets cheesed off that way and chicks dig it.  Social media is all abuzz about whose shirts you wear.

MT:  What?   The one time I wore my wife's shirt was because it was the only thing clean at the time and I was running late.   Who starts a meeting right at 9 AM?

GC: Oh. We were hoping to promote the "first cross-dresser in space" angle.  The public being a bit jaded and all...

MT:  I'm not a cross-dresser!

GC:  Hey, what you do in your personal time is your business.   We support you.  So how are you feeling?

MT:  A little annoyed at being called a "cross dresser!"

GC:  This is Ground Control to Major Tum.

MT:  Tom!

GC:  We need an official status report – something we could give to the media -- how are you feeling?

MT:  This is Major TOM to Ground Control – I'm floating in a most peculiar way.

GC:  Undergarments riding up on you?

MT:  And I can't reach them.

GC: That's why we did all those drills on weightlessness.   You didn't take a single Pilates class did, you?

MT:  No.

GC:  Yoga?

MT:  Please.  Not right after a protein bar.

GC:  YOU thought they were a waste of time but now you see the gravity of blowing them off, don't you?    So why DID you join the space program in the first place?

MT:  Grad school wasn't going well and I just needed to clear my head. Gain perspective.

GC:  So, what do you see?

MT:  The stars look very different today.

GC:  That's not much of a report.   We can't be telling taxpayers that their money went to fund a project where we learned "the stars look different in space."   We all figured that.

MT:  Planet Earth is blue.   Happy?

GC:  Not any better.   We all know that.

MT:  Well, there's nothing I can do.   It's all I've got for now.  You know, you sound like my wife always pumping me for details – (changes into high voice) "Is it gloss or is it semi-gloss?" (back to regular voice) Whatever!  (beat)... Aw, that's not fair to her – she's really great -- tell her I love her very much.

GC:  Roger that, Major Tum.

MT:  TOM!

GC:  I took the liberty of telling her that on my way in.

MT:  But she's at home.   It's her turn to bring snacks for the soccer team.

GC:  Oh, I just told this blond bombshell that I ASSUMED was your wife since she said she was here to see you.

MT:  That's not my wife!   This is how rumors get started.

GC:  Girlfriend, then?   Hey, what you do in your private life is not our concern.

MT:  No, Monica is a girl and a friend – but not (coughs on protein bar) my girlfriend!

GC:  What's that... you're breaking up....

MT:  My wife and I are not breaking up!

GC:  Are you eating candy over the instrument panel?

MT: No.

GC:  Sounds like you are.

MT:  It's a protein bar.   So it's sanctioned.

37

GC:  So she's not your girlfriend?

MT:  What's with the third degree here?  I already told you that...

GC:  Pretty hot.

MT:  You think so?  She's not really my type.

GC:  No, your intake manifold is running hot.

MT:  Uh...

GC:  The square thing above your head.

MT:  (feels above his head) This doo-hicky?  It feels ok to me.

GC:  Check the GAUGE – the numbers are hot – high – in the red zone?

MT:  Just a smidge -- is that bad?

GC:  Ground Control to Major Tom – your circuit's dead.  Is there something wrong?

MT:   You tell me!

GC:   Can you hear me, Major Tum?

MT:  Tom!  I hear you fine!

GC:  But your circuit's dead.... blimey!

MT:   And that means I should do what?   Or is there nothing I can do?

GC:  Yes, switch to auxiliary life support!

MT:  Ah...man, it's always something.

GC:  This is Ground Control to Major Tum – you MUST switch to auxiliary life support in the next 10 seconds or you will DIE!

MT:  I can't find the manual – not enough time to google it -- so many wires & buttons here...

GC:  Hit the OX  button now!

MT:  OX button?

GC:  Do it now!  Down to 3 seconds....

MT:  So you really think Monica is pretty?

GC:  You're out of oxygen.   You're DEAD!   Can you hear me, Major TOM?

MT:  Finally you get the name right and I'm dead.

GC: Yes, you're DEAD.  Or, as the Russian space program says, "kaputnik".  Time to leave the capsule.

MT:  I don't think I'm dead and I should know.  Why, I oughta ....

GC:  Don't blame the messenger.  You're dead – leave the capsule NOW!

(MAJOR TOM leaves Stage Right and crosses to Stage Left)

MT: Chillax, GC, it's just a simulation.   That's why we have 'em.   Live and learn.   You're only a failure when you stop trying.

GC (sarcastic):  Any other pearls of wisdom?

MT:  What doesn't kill you makes you stronger.

GC:  These simulations are expensive! Mission a complete failure!   Why can you not learn simple emergency procedures?

MT:  What's an OX button?   I never heard of that.

GC:  AUXILIARY Life Support button.   It's in BRIGHT GREEN to your right. How hard is that?

MT:  GREEN?   Why would you color an emergency button in green? That makes no sense.   It's very counter-intuitive.  If we have an emergency situation, I'm looking for a RED button.   And shouldn't it SAY "Auxiliary Life Support" instead of that stupid icon?

GC:  It shows a man – or woman – could be anyone – it's very gender neutral --doubled over.   There's not enough room for "Auxiliary Life Support" on the button.   The icon should be pretty self-explanatory.

MT:  OK, then how about "A.L.S."?

GC:  Really?  We're gonna have a button labeled with the disease Lou Gehrig died from?  We have people in Public Relations who think about that kind of stuff.

MT:  Lou Gehrig died of A.L.S ?

GC:  Yes!   What did you THINK he died of, you nimrod?

MT:  Duh!  Lou Gehrig's disease, you idiot.   It's like "Who is buried in Grant's tomb?".   It's a trick question.

GC:  Look it up and you'll find I'm right.   But that's why we have these simulations.   You don't always have time to THINK up there.   You need to be able to REACT.   We've had five simulations now and you've died in three of those.   So you're batting four hundred.    That's not good.

MT:  I think Lou Gehrig would disagree.

GC:  You clearly don't have the right stuff.   We're gonna get someone else.

MT:  I think with a few more simulations I can prove you wrong.

GC:  You're not getting ANY more simulations!

MT:  Calm down -- let's talk about it over lunch in the cafeteria – my treat.

GC:  I'm not budging on this!

MT:  With Monica.   I'll talk you up – tell her you taught me everything I know.

GC:  Another simulation tomorrow morning work for you?

 MT:  Sure!   Just not TOO early.

GC:  And Tom?  Sometime between now and then could you RTFM? (shoves loose-leaf binder into MT's hands)

# The Art of The Duel

Characters:    ALEX, male congressman who has been challenged to a duel

AARON, male congressman who challenged ALEX to a duel

DAWN, female, younger than ALEX/AARON, arbiter of duel

Props:   2 Pistols (preferably not real!), box that looks like it could carry 2 more pistols, laptop

Setting:   Clearing in the woods


(At rise, only DAWN and ALEX are on stage with ALEX pointing his pistol at DAWN.   DAWN is carrying a laptop and small box):

DAWN:  What do you think you're doing?

ALEX:  I'm here to preserve my honor.   What does it LOOK like?

DAWN:  But you're pointing your gun right at me.

ALEX:  "Pistols at Dawn".

DAWN:  I know that but...

ALEX: You're "Dawn", right?   Aaron told the arbitration agency that we didn't want a woman doing this but they insisted you'd be fine.

DAWN:  And I'll BE fine – this isn't my first rodeo.

ALEX (not impressed):   No Bull.   But this isn't a rodeo – this is a DUEL – if you're not up for this, now's the time to back out.

DAWN:  I AM up for this – but you can't be pointing your pistol at me. In fact, you shouldn't  ever point it at anything you're not planning at shooting.

ALEX:  I KNOW how to use a gun!

41

DAWN: I'm actually a firearms instructor and I don't think you do.  You sure know how to shoot your mouth off, though.

ALEX: I've watched a TON of Westerns so I know what I'm doing.

DAWN: And I've spent a lot of time listening to the Beach Boys but that doesn't mean I know how to surf!

ALEX: This may all be moot, though, if Aaron doesn't show up.

DAWN:  You mean "The 1st party"?   He challenged YOU so he's the 1st party and you're the 2nd party.

ALEX:  Well, I'm the first one here.  What happens if he doesn't show?

DAWN: American Standard rules of duel.

ALEX: Where you learned...

DAWN: In school.  He gets a 10-minute grace period and then he forfeits – your honor is intact, whereas HIS honor is impugned.   Is that him now?

(AARON runs onto the stage):   I'm here – traffic was miserable & mapquest screwed me.

DAWN:  Uh... no pistol?

ALEX  (to AARON):   Did you not even READ the contract?   BYOP. Bring Your Own Pistol  (To DAWN):  So does he forfeit now?

AARON (to ALEX): You'd LIKE to weasel out of this – I thought BYOP was "Bring Your Own Peeps".   I was GONNA bring my own pistol, though, but there's no way I can get to here from my house without going thru SOME school zone, government building, or whatever, and I didn't wanna get busted on the way over.   Arbiter has pistols, right? (Looking expectantly at DAWN).  I told you, Alex, no skirts!

DAWN:  I'm a VERY competent arbiter, thank you very much – and I have TWO pistols here (points to box).

AARON: Does your husband know you took his guns?

42

DAWN (a bit miffed): They're MINE – I bring them to every duel because I often run into a clown like you who isn't prepared. I'm a CERTIFIED arbiter. So man-up and accept the fact that I'm in charge here.

AARON: Yeah, well, maybe you should chick-up and lose the attitude. I thought you were supposed to be neutral.

DAWN: We're all here now so let's get started – First Party (nods at AARON), Second Party (nods at ALEX).

AARON (nods formally towards ALEX): Two.

ALEX (nods formally towards AARON): One.

DAWN: Good! Now, let's go over the terms of the duel.

AARON: It's real simple – person who dies, loses.

DAWN: Will you let me do my job? Why did you even BOTHER hiring an arbiter if you're not going to allow her to do due diligence?

AARON: What's this about "doodoo diligence"?

ALEX: Let's let her do her job, Aaron.

AARON: Call me "One" – we're keeping this all legal!

ALEX (sighs): Let's let her do her job, ONE.

DAWN: Thank you, TWO.

AARON (to ALEX): Suck up!

DAWN: First order of business is to point out that tree over there with the target on it. Should either of you want to NOT shoot the other but STILL keep your honor, you can shoot at that target. Don't just shoot in the air – I know it SEEMS honorable – but it's also extremely reckless.

AARON: Don't you mean "grossly negligent"?

DAWN: Either way, it leaves us ALL open to the possibility of a lawsuit.

ALEX: Except for the dead person.

43

AARON:  Can I look at the pistols in the box?

DAWN:   You're jumping ahead a bit, One, but OK (opens the box for AARON to peer in).

AARON:  Those are some fine guns.  Didn't bring a sharpie, though, did you?

DAWN: What for?

AARON:  So I can make SURE that the bullet has HIS name on it.

DAWN:  We'll all know if you shoot him but go ahead and both of you make sure that your pistols are to your liking.

AARON:  I think HIS is DOUBLE action and both of yours are SINGLE action!

DAWN:  Doesn't matter.   You're each using only one bullet.   After the bullet is discharged, the duel is over.

AARON:  What if he goes on a shooting rampage?  He'll have the advantage.

ALEX:  I'm not gonna go on a shooting spree.

AARON:  I said "rampage".

ALEX:  Either one — This duel was YOUR idea, remember?

DAWN:  And if he DOES go on a shooting spree --

ALEX:  Or rampage...

DAWN:  He loses his honor and YOU win by forfeit.

AARON:  But I'll be dead.

DAWN:  But you'll have your honor and he will irrevocably lose his. That's what this is all about, right?

AARON:  He smeared my name and so I must restore my honor!

DAWN:  Uh, this is not really my purview but how did Two insult you?

AARON:  With a racial slur!  He said I should be blackballed from the committee.

DAWN:  That's it?  That's not really a...

AARON:  And then he said my speeches all sounded like "White Noise". More racism!

ALEX:  Hey, YOU were the one who made a sexist comment – saying that I was guilty of "malfeasance".

DAWN:  I don't think any of this should reasonably be construed as....

ALEX:  And THEN you smeared my constituents, saying they were a "homogeneous bunch".

DAWN (incredulous):  And THIS is worth a duel?  Unbelievable!

AARON:  Hey, just do your job and stay neutral.

DAWN:  Oh, I'm neutral, all right – I think you're both equal idiots.

ALEX:  Can we just get on with this?  I know we're paying you by the hour.

DAWN:  And I've got a soccer game to referee in 2 hours so, ok, if I can go over the terms without any further interruption (looks at laptop).  We're ok with the pistols and the "no-loss-of-honor target".  How about the "DNR" clause?

AARON:  If I get shot by TWO, here, I don't want you waking me up.  Just let me die rather than live the rest of my days in disgrace.

DAWN:  But what if you get shot in, say, the thigh?

AARON:  I think we're all adults here...(Looks towards ALEX)... Two?

ALEX:  Agreed, here, One – it's up to the party who is injured to ask for help -- IF he wants it.

DAWN:  No loss of honor, then?

AARON:  Only if he uses The Lord's name in vain.

ALEX:  Agreed.   And, while we're at it, let's say that ALL profanity is grounds for forfeit and loss of honor.

AARON:  With you on that, Two.

DAWN:  OK, we're making great progress here.   So you start back-to-back and then count off 10 steps.

AARON:  SIMULTANEOUSLY!

ALEX:  And SLOWLY.   No fast count!

DAWN:  Simultaneously and slowly.   You then turn in whichever direction – clockwise or counter – and then you're free to fire at either the other party or the NLOH target.

AARON (to ALEX):  NLOH ?

ALEX (to AARON):  No Loss of Honor.   Learn the lingo, will you?

DAWN:  Once you hear "Ten", you're free to turn and fire – a common misconception is that you have to wait for the word "Turn" but that's actually not true.

ALEX:  Good to know.

AARON:  Let's DO this!

DAWN:  One last thing – the matter of "time outs".   Each side is allowed ONE timeout during the CTT...

AARON (to ALEX):  CTT ?

ALEX:  "Count To Ten".   You don't know the terminology?   I thought you said you've dueled before.

AARON:  I have!   And I'm undefeated!

DAWN:  OK, are we ALL on board with the terms here?    One?

AARON (to ALEX, looking at Alex's shoes):  You and your pumped-up kicks can't out-run my bullet.

DAWN:   A simple "Yes" will suffice here.

AARON: Yes!

DAWN: Two?

ALEX: Yes 'm.

DAWN: OK, stand back-to-back (ALEX & AARON comply with this at center stage). Here we go!

ALEX: WAIT!

AARON: What?

ALEX: My back is itchy. (To AARON): You scratch my back ... I'll scratch yours.

AARON: Mine's not itchy.

ALEX: This is gonna drive me crazy – it's the cold, dry air.

AARON (muttering): Oh, for the love of... (scratches ALEX's back very hurriedly).

ALEX: To the left just a bit... ok, you got it... thanks!

DAWN: Are we ready now? Back to back w/ pistols pointing upward (ALEX & AARON comply). Here's our re-start... God speed... and may good sportsmanship prevail.

DAWN/AARON/ALEX (ALEX & AARON each take a step with each number): ONE, TWO, THREE, FOUR...

ALEX (reaching in pocket annoyed): TIME OUT! TIME OUT!

AARON (stops counting/walking): Oh, what is this? You already had your one time out!

DAWN: Technically, that was a "re-start" – it was before the CTT. Time out is granted.

ALEX: I gotta take this.

AARON: Really?

ALEX: It might be my last one... (into phone).   Yeah, I just wanted to get some work done and some fresh air.... I haven't forgotten about the milk.... Uh, one thing...

AARON (reaches into his pocket and starts talking into his phone):   It's about honor ... I know you won't...

ALEX (into phone):   I can't explain but... I MIGHT be late...I'm sure it will turn up....

AARON (into phone):   Yeah, well, I just assumed you'd be more supportive (turns off phone).

ALEX (into phone):   I gotta go – don't wanna get fired on.   What?  Oh, reception is bad... don't wanna get fired ....gotta go... bye (hangs up).

DAWN (impatient after all this):   Are we ready now?

AARON:   Hey, Dawn, you seem to be in a hurry.   We can save you some time, dispense w/ the CTT, and both just fire at the target.   No loss of honor for anyone.   OK by you, Two?

ALEX (puzzled but relieved):   OK by me, One!

AARON:   So, Madame Arbiter, there's no need for you to even supervise – we'll share One's pistol, shoot at the target, and we're done.   You'll still get paid for the full hour.

DAWN:   We're already into the second hour.

AARON:   Fine, fine – we'll pay you for the second hour and gas money – right, One?

ALEX (still relieved):   Uh, sure – it's taxpayer money anyway so who cares?

AARON:   Right – part of our ongoing investigation into... where is your family from, Dawn?

DAWN:  I was born here.   My father is from England if that helps.

ALEX:  Need somewhere more ominous.

DAWN:  I visited Latvia one time.  Does that help?

AARON:  Perfect!   Investigation into Latvian meddling.

ALEX:  "Influence"!

AARON:  And peddling.   Meddling and Peddling.

ALEX:  It's a bit unsettling.

DAWN:   As a taxpayer, I know I should be outraged  but I'm just glad to get the hell out of here.

AARON:  Language!   Do you talk to those soccer kids with that mouth?

ALEX:  Yeah, you never know if someone's kid will show up at one of these duels or see it on Instagram.

DAWN:  Sorry – ok, enjoy the rest of your morning (walks off stage shaking her head).

ALEX (to AARON):  So why the change of heart?   Realize it was all a misunderstanding?

AARON:   No, uh...I don't know if I should tell you this....no loss of honor, remember!   It's a bit embarrassing.

ALEX:  Ah ha!   You were talking to your wife on the phone too!   She wouldn't let you do it!

AARON:  My wife couldn't care less.

ALEX (sobered by this):  Oh.   That's actually pretty sad.   Sorry to hear that, dude.

AARON:  Girlfriend, though – that's a different story.

# The Cat In the Hat Takes Flak

Characters:   NICK (male, the younger the better)

SALLY (female, Nick's sister, the younger the better)

THE CAT IN THE HAT (TCITH, male or female any age)

BART (male, in 30's-60's, works for Social Services)

Props:  2 shovels, photo of SALLY/NICK's mom, long red & white hat for TCITH, clipboard for BART to take notes for Social Services.

Setting: Just outside NICK/SALLY's house

At rise:   NICK, SALLY, TCITH are surveying the situation outside the house, BART is off-stage


NICK (leaning on shovel):   It has been a long day.

SALLY (leaning on shovel):   With no time to play.

NICK: Yet we have a big task that remains undone.

TCITH: But why the long faces when we've had so much fun?

SALLY (to TCITH):  When it comes to cleaning, you do not know thing one.

NICK (to TCITH):  So to ease Sally's nervousness, I called Social Services (gestures to BART, who enters from Stage Left).

TCITH:  This is something I do not understand.   We have the situation well in hand.

BART:  I say that I will be the judge of that.   I have heard of your mischief, Cat in the Hat.   Now you will whine that you are misunderstood.   But the fact of the matter is you're up to no good. You, Cat, should never come around.   All you do is bring property values down.  (To NICK):  It was wise to call me and tell me the matter.

SALLY:  I told him to do it, though we have limited data.

BART:  You both are smart kids, that I can tell.  Your mother was wise to give you a cell.  My name is Bart, a name you should love because I'm here to help you – I work for the gov.

TCITH:  Now, Bart, I say you should hold your horses.  I know how you hose us in Human Resources.

BART:  I am not in H.R., but I think you know that.  You should not start rumors, Cat in the Hat.

TCITH:  So, you work for the gov; then, let me guess, Bart.  You could not pass math and flunked out of art.

BART:  I know, Cat, that you think I'm boring and dumb.  But I, sir, am here to solve a conundrum.  So, try to avoid any insults or scuffle.  Someone tell me how we got in this kerfuffle.

NICK:  When mom left for the day, she gave us a job.  To shovel the snow -- our neighbor is a snob.

BART:  But my records show you should be okay.  You are not encumbered by an H.O.A.

SALLY:  We started to work, and we did not shirk.

NICK:  We spent the morning trying so hard.  It is a back-breaking chore to clear up our yard.  Then soon along came the Cat in the Hat.  I knew he was trouble – I smelled a rat.

TCITH:  It was a most ambitious endeavor.  Do you not have tools, not even a lever?

SALLY:  He had been here before, about a year and a half.  We let him in then and it sure was no laugh.

TCITH:  Now, Nick and Sally, you make a great fuss.  But please do not throw me under the bus.

NICK:  You came in the house without bothering to knock.

TCITH:  Have you ever thought of changing your lock?

SALLY (to BART):   The first thing Cat did was eat cake in the tub.    I told him quite plainly to find his own grub.

TCITH:  Not to be picky, but it was pie a-la-mode.

NICK:  What does it matter?  That's such a pant load!

BART:  So, the Cat in that Hat stayed in the tub until?

NICK:  He finished the cake and ran up our water bill.

SALLY:  When the Cat left the tub, we saw a big ring.   And that, to our mom, is a very big thing.   A ring is something we did not seek.  When our mom gets home, boy, would she freak!

NICK:  So, to get rid of the ring, the cat used mom's slit skirt.

TCITH:  I thought I was smart – I was being alert.   Now, you all make me feel pretty hurt.

BART:  Okay, it might be time for some confession.   Is your mom working in the oldest profession?   Do you have some form of photo ID?    I want to be thorough so I really should see.

NICK (hands photo to BART):  She gave me this photo and Sally one just the same.   After our dad left, she wanted to prove she had game.

BART (impressed with photo):  I will have to say that she is a cutie – a pretty face and check out that booty.    So, she still looks like that?   I want to avoid confusion.

NICK:  Some favorable lighting but it is not an illusion.

BART:  One more question and I do not want to be rude.   Has she ever once identified as a dude?

SALLY:  It is great that you like her and find her so pretty.   But, she's coming home soon from her trip to the city.   So if you want to impress her and show her you care, let us finish the story, as we're getting nowhere.

NICK: So, the skirt was dirt.

SALLY: How could she flirt?

NICK: That Cat has gall. He goes into the hall and beats the skirt on the wall.

TCITH: So, we cleaned up the skirt and cleaned up the wall. If you want my opinion, we were having a ball.

SALLY: You cleaned up the wall at the expense of her shoes. I wouldn't want to tell her that bit of news.

NICK: Then we thought "Is this cat on some drug?" He wiped off the shoes on Dad's old rug.

BART: This is intriguing, and I am glad you called. So, are you telling me that your father is bald? It is surprising he left his toupee. The plot thickens, that I must say.

NICK: No, our father has hair – but why should you care? This was a long floor rug.

SALLY: One our parents both dug.

TCITH: But I cleaned up the rug by using the bed.

SALLY: With the spot on the bed, we'd be better off dead.

BART: Now I can understand all your frustration. But please tell me you did not take her medication. Perhaps we can work out some compensation?

NICK: With the spot on the bed, matters came to a head.

TCITH: In all fairness, it was the wrong kind of bed.

SALLY (fed up and mocking TCITH's voice): "Wrong kind of bed?". That's what he said!

NICK: So just when things had reached the worst, he recruits three more cats – I think we are cursed. He brings in little cats A, B, and C. What if they vomit, what if they pee?

TCITH: And those cats got the spot out of the house.  So, I see no reason for you to say I am a louse.    The spot is gone – that is what you wanted.  The way you kids howl, you'd think the house haunted.

NICK: But the spot is not gone – just check out our lawn.

TCITH: Yes, the snow is pink.    But why the big stink?    It's kind of fancy, do you not think?

NICK: Could you be more obtuse?  Could you be even duller?   We can't live in a house where the snow is that color.

SALLY (to TCITH): Why can you not see that this cannot be good?  We'll be pariahs in our own neighborhood.

NICK: We'll have to scramble; we'll have to retreat.

SALLY: We might have to move to Mulberry Street.

NICK (to TCITH): I know that you're older and you're only old once.    But I cannot believe that you are such a dunce.

TCITH: You need to chillax, kids, and learn to mellow.    It is not like the lawn is a pale shade of yellow.    You will get used to it – it might take endurance.    It is probably covered in your homeowner's insurance.

BART: I agree with the Cat here  – now how about that?    But he shouldn't be praised, and he shouldn't be petted.    Never let him in a house – until fully vetted.    But the house is clean?

TCITH: It is pristine.

SALLY: We cannot live with pink snow!  What will we do?  Where will we go?

TCITH: If all else fails, you can live with me.  Oh, the places you'll go; the places you'll see!

NICK: I still want to try this thing you call "Voom."    Otherwise, we face certain doom.    I do not want to be sent to my room.

BART: Voom is new to me.    How good can it be?

TCITH:  It is in the possession of little cat Z.

NICK:  Yeah, we skipped just a bit of the story – 25 cats in all of their glory.

SALLY:  That's not hunky-dory.

BART:  25 cats, why that cannot be!  (To TCITH):  Surely, you got a snippity-dee-dee.

TCITH:  I'm pretty buff and I'm pretty burly.   So I'll ask you now to not call me "Shirley".  But Voom can make the snow all white.   If you use it now, your future is bright.   I do not want to quarrel; I do not want to fight.   All I want to do is set things right.

BART (to TCITH) :  I want to help and be your buddy.   But has Voom been tested in a double-blind study?

TCITH:  We want to get rid of the pink, I think.   So let us try Voom and do not be a dink.   You work in the gov with all of the perks.   Yet all you do is gum up the works.

BART:  You might think all is fine and okay.   But it hasn't been approved by the F.D.A.

TCITH:  I know that a clean lawn the family  would savor. So do me a favor and let me just sign a waiver.

BART:  We need to be legal and it is not that simple.   We're clearing a yard, not removing a pimple.

TCITH:  We don't want mom mad; we don't want to shame her.   Why can't I  sign a simple disclaimer?  Kids, what do you say – are you all for tryin'?   I don't want to do this without your buy-in.

SALLY:  I say that we give Voom a try.  I know that pink snow would make our mom cry.

NICK:  So, let's use it here and use it now.   If mom sees pink snow, she'll have a cow.

SALLY:  (primarily to BART):  Yes, let's  use Voom to clean up this mess. Mom will thank you and she is the one you want to impress.

BART: Is she seeing someone?   I probably should ask.

SALLY: One guy so ugly, he should wear a mask!

NICK: Dad could be weird – he had a few quirks.   But the men mom dates are losers or jerks.   So, you have nothing to fear – the path is quite clear.   You should know that we both hold her quite dear, even though we've portrayed her to be a pain in the rear.

SALLY: So, how about we close this whole deal.   Then, Bart, you can meet Mom and share a hot meal!

TCITH: I know you all want me to soon go away.  So, we will use Voom and call it a day.   I know I'm not invited but I do have one wish.   Would you be kind and  give my little cats a dish?   They all fit in my hat so they must not get fat.   Would you be a good gal, Sal, and make it low-cal?

SALLY: We have just the thing – you will find it delish.   "One fish, two fish, red fish, blue fish!"

# The Straight Dope

Characters:    JEFF: college student  somewhat-slightly built, average height

BOB:  college student , slightly shorter, good friend of Jeff

VERONICA:  Pretty college girl, friend of Bob, knows Jeff only thru Bob

ALICIA:   Very attractive college girl, acquaintance of Jeff & Bob

Stage Requirements/props:

Short park bench that characters can drift on and off, as conversation dictates.

( At rise, BOB and VERONICA are sitting on a bench.   JEFF and ALICIA are off stage)

VERONICA:  So where WERE you last night?

BOB: I decided to hang out with Biff.

VERONICA (disappointed):  I waited for you in the library for hours.   I had to finish the paper myself.

BOB: Sorry about that.   I'll make it up to you.

VERONICA: Well, the paper is DONE now.    You know,  I never thought I'd say this, but it was a good thing Jeff showed up.

BOB: I never thought ANYONE would say that either  -- you've always said he's a pig.

VERONICA:  Yeah, he's still a bit of a pig -- but he sure saved me last night in the library.

BOB: From what?

VERONICA:  These two guys were really giving me a hard time.

BOB: So who was the other guy with Jeff?

VERONICA:  No, these two guys I'd never seen before were hassling me. Then Jeff  showed up,  said something to the guys that I'd rather not repeat, and they both took off after him.

BOB: Jeff's such a coward.   I'll bet he ran.

VERONICA: Those were two BIG guys.   They probably chased Jeff clear across campus.   But it gave me the perfect opportunity to get away.

BOB: That's him coming up now.    Looks like he survived the pummeling.

(Jeff walks up to the bench, thrilled to see Veronica, who's not as thrilled to see him)

JEFF (very cheerful) :   Hey, guys!

BOB & VERONICA (less enthusiastically):   Hey.

JEFF (undeterred):  You  sure look happy.

BOB: We both just finished our papers on the Agricultural Revolution. The professor gave us a tight deadline & he can be very critical.

JEFF (trying to be funny): I hear he's outstanding in his field.

(Bob & Veronica just groan & look at each other, hoping Jeff will just leave)

JEFF (mostly to Veronica):  Get it?   It's a decent pun.   I mean, I've done better...

VERONICA (somewhat grudgingly):  I really should thank you, Jeff for bailing me out last night.   Bob was supposed to meet me but was hanging out with Biff.   Are you ok?

JEFF: Oh, yeah, I left those guys in the dust.   In the words of Eric Carmen, "I'm a marathon man".

VERONICA: Uh, don't you mean Dustin Hoffman?

JEFF: Oh, the movie -- yeah, CLASSIC movie -- but the song is even better. I could play it for you, sometime, Veronica.   I think you'd like it.   Yeah, Bob, I know -- you're not  impressed.

BOB: Whoop dee, he's a  marathon man.   So what?

JEFF: It's about a guy finding his identity. (very passionate)   Eric Carmen is the best at that.   He also writes great songs about disillusionment.

BOB: Sorry, Jeff -- normally, we could put up with this trivia but I've got things I need to get done & don't have  time to waste.

VERONICA (completely ignoring Jeff):   Bob, I can handle some of it. Gambrell isn't too far out of my way home.

BOB (also ignoring Jeff):   You've already run errands for me.   I couldn't ask you to do another one.

JEFF:   Hey, I could help out.

VERONICA (still ignoring Jeff):   It's not a big deal.

BOB (still ignoring Jeff): I know -- but I never do anything for you & it IS out of the way.

VERONICA:   Well, I need the exercise anyway.

JEFF (pouncing on opportunity to get back in the conversation):   You don't need the exercise, Veronica!   In fact, I think you've lost weight since the last time I saw you (goes up to Veronica , half-way tries to gently pinch her behind).   (very playfully)  Gitchy Gitchy.

VERONICA (easily side-steps Jeff & says to Bob):   I'll drop off your paper at Gambrell.

JEFF:  You can pinch me if it'll make you feel better.

VERONICA:  It would NOT make me feel better.

JEFF:  Are you sure?   I'd make ME feel better -- give it the old  "gitchy gitchy" (sticks out his rear end).

BOB (realizing he'd better step in to intervene):   OK, Veronica, it WOULD really help me to not have to go cross-campus again.

JEFF:  Hey, Veronica, I could go with you.   It's getting a bit dark, wouldn't hurt to have an escort.   Seriously, I won't try anything -- you know that.

VERONICA (not sure how to take Jeff here):   I know that but...Um, no thanks.  It's not a big deal.  See ya, Bob.   (Gives Bob a hug that Bob isn't as enthusiastic about returning & then walks off).

JEFF (softly to Bob):  Where's MY hug?

BOB:  You want a hug?

JEFF:  Not from you.   From her!   She is SO pretty!

BOB:  She's cute.

JEFF:  She's fantastic!  And smart too!   She always tries to help you out...not sure how you could do better.

BOB (sighs): Yeah, she's a nice girl

JEFF:  I'm no expert on chicks -- but it looks to me like she's lobbying hard to be your girlfriend.

BOB:  Yeah, I know.

JEFF:  Yet you'd rather hang out with Biff?

BOB: I just told Veronica that.    I was actually at a party with people who are more interesting and can help me more with my career.   Biff was there too so technically I wasn't lying.

JEFF:  So you're playing hard to get.    I don't know how you do it but it sure seems to work.   Worked great with Eleanor   Why did you dump her anyway?   She was pretty decent.

BOB:  Eleanor became too clingy.

JEFF:  I think she just wanted you to spend more time with her.

BOB:  Monogamy is overrated.

JEFF:  Oh, no!  Monogamy is UNDERrated!  Now, CELIBACY is overrated.

BOB:  Celibacy is NOT overrated.

JEFF:  Are you kidding?  Celibacy sucks!

BOB:  Yeah, but we all KNOW that -- something is not "overrated" unless there are people who actually think it's great.

JEFF:  At one time, wasn't it considered "holy" to be celibate?  So SOME people must've thought it was a great thing.  It doesn't take a genius to know that those guys were idiots.

BOB (a bit impatient):  Only an idiot would think you're a genius, Jeff.  But yes, I think we're in agreement here that celibacy sucks.  Monogamy gets complicated, though.

JEFF:  Only that one time when you were dating Darlene.  She was quite the demando ...

BOB:  Yeah, you guys sure called that one.  Having actually BEEN in a few relationships now, I can tell you that committing to ONE girl is more trouble than it's worth.

JEFF:  I've never been in one but I'd like to test that theory with Veronica.

BOB:  She's ok -- but that's it.  Doesn't do much for me.

JEFF:  So you're not gonna ask her out?

BOB:  Nope, not  my type.

JEFF:  Well, then you really oughta TELL her.  You OWE her some honesty after all she's done for you.

BOB:  And how has the honesty policy worked for you, Jeff?  Had any dates that weren't inflatable?

JEFF:  I sent it back -- I told you that!

BOB: Only when you found out the price didn't include shipping.

JEFF: Veronica, however, is NOT inflatable & you're taking advantage of her.   You should let her know that you don't share her feelings.

BOB (irritated):   Yes!   I'll tell her soon!

JEFF: I don't know why you haven't told her already.   She's a very sweet girl who deserves better.

BOB (angry): If she wants to run errands for me, why should you care? This doesn't concern you!

JEFF:  In a way it does.   I don't wanna  violate the code.

BOB (cooling down):  Huh?

JEFF:  Well, I only know Veronica through you so that puts her squarely onto your turf.

BOB:  Turf?   What are you talking about?

JEFF:  We're men!   We're hunters!   It's how we were created.   We're hunting for the right girl!   Some more successfully than others.   But I don't want to jeopardize our friendship by asking out a girl who's on your turf...

BOB:  Nobody hunts on "turf".   Maybe you mean ..."safari"?

JEFF:  Whatever metaphor that will work here.   I would never betray you.   I've never violated the code & I never will!

BOB:   I've never HEARD of the code but if it makes you feel better, I won't betray you that way either.

JEFF:   Hey, thanks!     It did happen to me one time & it was very painful. So ... just to be clear then,  you'd be ok if I asked out Veronica?

BOB:   Sure, I'd have no problem with it.

JEFF:  No regrets or resentment if we fall madly in love and get married? She could be the one -- a pretty girl who's not too hung up on looks.

BOB:  How do you know that?

JEFF:   As a rule, a girl of Veronica's caliber only wants to date big athletic types like, say, your friend Biff.   Yet she's interested in you.   No offense, but I think I'm at least as attractive as you are.   Therefore, I gotta like my chances with her.

BOB (taken aback):   What makes you say that?

JEFF:  Well, I'm a bit taller, haven't lost as much hair and I work out 3 times a week.   I'm benching more than my body weight.

BOB:  That's not what it's all about.

JEFF:   Yeah, I think girls like abs & biceps too.   So I've stepped up the curls & crunches.   But I officially have your permission to date her?

BOB:   For what it's worth...

JEFF (very encouraged):   Cool!   That makes my day!

BOB:   You're wasting your time, though.

JEFF:  Why?   You said you weren't interested & she obviously doesn't have a boyfriend.

BOB:   That doesn't mean she'll go out with you.

JEFF:  After you tell her you're not interested, yeah, she may be broken up a bit.  So you could throw in a good word about me.   You don't want her to think you're just trying to UNLOAD her.   Just let her know that you're not interested but I am -- and that I'm a good guy who works out 3 times a week and my intentions are completely honorable.

BOB:  She despises you.

JEFF (completely surprised):  What?   How do you know?

BOB:   She's told me.

JEFF:  She never told ME!

BOB:  Well, she HAS told me.   Several times.   She can't stomach you.

JEFF (devastated): But my intentions are honorable!   I've got a good future ahead of me.   And I work out 3 times a week.   I just don't get it!

BOB:  Jeff, you know what your problem with women is?

JEFF:  They don't like me.

BOB:  Do you wanna  know or not?

JEFF:  Like you're some expert.

BOB:  I get a lot more interest than you do.

JEFF (contrite & eager to learn):   OK, I'm listening.   So really, it's just ONE problem?

BOB:  Your  ONE problem with women is: The moment you see an attractive girl, you think about having sex with her.

JEFF:  Well, yeah ...duh!  (sarcastic)  I'm SO ashamed.   Bring in the shrink!   Whaddaya expect?  I'm a straight guy!

BOB:  You're a straight dope!   You're doomed from the get-go.

JEFF:  Hey,  looks are the first thing I see!   I'm not gonna  break her heart.   I'm willing to wait till she's ready -- even if that's not till we're married.   But EVENTUALLY I want....well... sexual healing.

BOB (knows what's coming):  Oh, no.   Not the Marvin.

JEFF (singing & doing his best impersonation of Marvin Gaye).   When I get this feeling I want sexual healing (forgetting most of the words).   Blah blah blah blah blah  ...    I got sick this morning.... um, temperature rising...

BOB:  You can't sing.   At least learn the lyrics.   But you can't get your advice on women from Marvin.

JEFF:  You know, I always thought Marvin Gaye was over-rated until I heard that song.   If he were alive today & I met him, I'd tell him, "Marve, that song says it all."   It really sucks he's dead.

BOB: Didn't he get shot by a jealous lover?   Or was it the girl in the video?

JEFF: No!   It was his dad, you idiot!   I can't believe I'm taking advice on women from someone who doesn't know how Marvin Gaye died.

BOB: I DO know you can't sing "Sexual Healing" to girls when you meet 'em.   Don't even THINK it.

JEFF: But I don't think I'm wrong about the sex thing.   Women want to get married.   Men need some motivation -- otherwise, we're just  doing chores for nothing.   Sex IS a major reason for men to want to get married.   It is for me, anyway.   Doesn't the bible say somewhere about "getting married so you won't burn with passion"?

BOB: I think it's in Corinthians or something.   I learned it in Sunday School years ago.

JEFF:   OK, let's say I AM thinking about it -- how do THEY KNOW I'm thinking about it?

BOB:  They just do.   It PROBABLY doesn't help when you look like you wanna  pinch them & say things like "gitchy gitchy".

JEFF: Really?   I don't get that.   It wouldn't bother me if a woman tried that & said "gitchy gitchy".   I could go for it right now, in fact (looks around to see if there's anyone nearby).

BOB: Women are not men.

JEFF:   I mean, even if she were HIDEOUSLY ugly, or  I just didn't like her, I STILL would be somewhat flattered.

BOB (mock admiration):  That's very egalitarian of you.

JEFF:  But you're saying that girls don't want me thinking about sex when I meet  them?

BOB:  Correct!

JEFF:  That's hard to believe.   And a bit unrealistic  on their part.   OK, what SHOULD I think about?

BOB: Anything else is better. Push the sex thoughts to the very back of your mind.

JEFF (incredulous): And YOU can do that? You can meet a real hottie & NOT think, "Ooh, I'll bet she'd cross her ankles just in the right spot on my back."

BOB: You think about THAT?

JEFF: Uh, yeah, I like feeling buckled in. You DON'T think about that?

BOB: No! It's called "being mature. " And you've seen the results.

JEFF: Yeah, the data don't lie. Neither will Veronica, apparently. You can't get her to reconsider?

BOB: Afraid not. First impressions are big & she thinks you're a pig.

JEFF (mulling): OK, next time I meet an attractive woman, I'll try real hard to not think about sex.

BOB: That's ALL there is to it.

JEFF: It won't be easy but it's worth a try.... seems unnatural, though. Maybe I'll think about the Agricultural Revolution.

BOB: If that's what it takes for you to not soil yourself.

JEFF: Hey, that's pretty good! You're all right, Bob! You've given me a lot to think about. All this time I've been a jerk (very discouraged).

BOB (quieter to Jeff): Here's your chance to be the "new you" -- looks like Alicia is coming our way -- though she's out of your league. Steady, boy...no drooling.

(Alicia walks by the bench where Bob is still sitting. Jeff stands to allow her room on the bench w/ Bob)

ALICIA (joking) Bob and Jeff -- that can only mean trouble.

BOB: I'm trying to keep HIM out of any.

ALICIA: I see you two having these "meaning of life" talks on this bench all the time -- sometimes with one or two other guys -- and I've often wondered what they're about.  So what deep discussion has it been THIS time?

BOB:  Jeff was talking about sexual healing.

JEFF (a bit defensive & still discouraged):  The SONG -- by Marvin Gaye.

ALICIA:  I remember it well.

BOB:  Jeff, here, thinks it's some sort of masterpiece.

ALICIA (mulling a bit):  I always liked it.  Actually, it IS a terrific song.

JEFF (softly):  It really is.

ALICIA:  Wasn't it the last big hit he had?

JEFF:  Yeah, right before...

ALICIA:  His idiot father shot him.   I still remember exactly where I was when I heard the news.

JEFF:  Me too!

BOB (a bit annoyed and dismissive):  Whatever...

ALICIA:  Anyway, Jeff, you're just the guy I'm looking for!   I was hoping you could help me with my paper on the Industrial Revolution.

JEFF (still discouraged & nods at Bob):  There's your guy.   I don't know much about anything.

BOB:   Industrial Revolution?   I'm your guy, Alicia.   Jeff barely got off the assembly line.

ALICIA:  Bob, you're a bit of a tool.   Jeff, you've always been honest -- I know you'll give me the straight dope on my paper.

JEFF (a bit encouraged):  Yeah, I can do that.

ALICIA:  I've always seen you speak your mind and I've admired  that -- it takes guts to not just tell everyone what they wanna hear all the time.

JEFF (more comfortable):  I just try to call 'em as I see 'em and it's what I want from everyone else.

ALICIA: Great!  Let's go then!   I made too much dinner for one anyway. You like spaghetti?

JEFF: (very encouraged):  Who doesn't?  OK, I guess I'm ready when you are!

(both start to walk off together as Bob is dumbfounded)

ALICIA (singing):  When I get that feeling, I want sexual healing....

JEFF (surprised & then tentatively trying to sing with her):  Makes me feel so fine... uh...

 ALICIA (singing):  Helps release my mind....

 (both are now offstage)

JEFF:  Uh, Alicia?

ALICIA:  Yeah?

JEFF:  Did you just "gitchy gitchy" me?